WILDLIFE AT RISK

TIGERS

Helen Riley

The Bookwright Press
New York • 1990

Wildlife at Risk

Bears Elephants
Birds of Prey Tigers

Cover An Indian tigress resting in the shade.

First published in the
United States in 1990 by
The Bookwright Press
387 Park Avenue South
New York, NY 10016

First published in 1990 by
Wayland (Publishers) Ltd
61 Western Road, Hove,
East Sussex, BN3 1JD, England

© Copyright 1990 Wayland (Publishers) Ltd

Library of Congress Cataloging-in-Publication Data

Riley, Helen.
    Tigers / by Helen Riley.
        p. cm. – (Wildlife at Risk)
    Includes bibliographical references.
    Summary: Discusses the physical characteristics,
habitat, behavior, and endangered nature of the Tiger.
    ISBN 0–531–18355–6
    1. Tigers – Juvenile literature. [1. Tigers. 2. Rare animals.
3. Wildlife conservation.] I. Title. II. Series.
    Library of Congress Card No. 90–690 1990.

Typeset by R. Gibbs & N. Taylor, Wayland
Printed in Italy by L.E.G.O. S.p.A., Vicenza

Contents

All words printed in **bold** are explained
in the glossary on page 30.

INTRODUCTION

Almost everyone has seen a tiger in a zoo. But few people have seen a wild tiger. In fact, we are very lucky still to have the chance of seeing a wild tiger. Only twenty years ago, these beautiful striped cats were in serious danger of becoming **extinct**.

The map shows where tigers lived in the past and where they live today. We know from old stories and **fossil** remains that many tigers once lived throughout the huge continent of Asia.

A magnificent Indian tiger photographed in the wild.

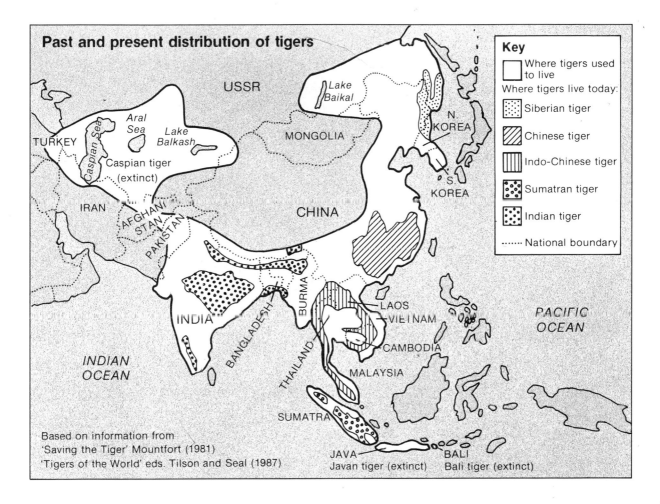

Past and present distribution of tigers

USSR

Lake Baikal

Aral Sea

Lake Balkash

TURKEY

Caspian Sea

Caspian tiger (extinct)

MONGOLIA

N. KOREA

S. KOREA

IRAN

AFGHANI-STAN

PAKISTAN

CHINA

INDIA

BANGLADESH

BURMA

THAILAND

LAOS

VIETNAM

CAMBODIA

MALAYSIA

PACIFIC OCEAN

INDIAN OCEAN

SUMATRA

JAVA — Javan tiger (extinct)

BALI — Bali tiger (extinct)

Key

☐ Where tigers used to live

Where tigers live today:

▦ Siberian tiger

▨ Chinese tiger

▥ Indo-Chinese tiger

▨ Sumatran tiger

▨ Indian tiger

······ National boundary

Based on information from
'Saving the Tiger' Mountfort (1981)
'Tigers of the World' eds. Tilson and Seal (1987)

You can see from the map that there are far fewer tigers alive today. We can only guess how many tigers used to live in Asia, but it must have been many hundreds of thousands. We do know that between 1930 and 1970 the total world **population** of tigers fell from about 100,000 down to about 5,000. If this worrying fall in numbers had continued, then tigers would very soon have become extinct.

This book tells the story of the tiger. It explains how tigers live, and how they were saved from extinction. It also looks at what still needs to be done to ensure that tigers will survive in the future.

THE TIGER FAMILY

Tigers are the largest members of the **cat family**. Other **species** of cats related to tigers include lions and leopards, and also the domestic cats that many of us keep as pets.

There are eight kinds of tigers, which are all listed in the data box. We call each different kind of tiger a **subspecies**. Three subspecies of tigers have recently become extinct. They are the Bali tiger, the Javan tiger and the Caspian tiger.

White tigers are not a separate subspecies, but a rare kind of Indian tiger with a pale coat and blue eyes.

A Siberian tiger.

Siberian tigers live in the very cold cedar forests of northern Asia. They are the largest of the tigers and have pale, yellowish fur. As you travel south, the subspecies of tigers become smaller.

Today most tigers live in the forests of Southeast Asia. Some live in areas of grassland or in marshy swamps. All tigers need thick bushes to hide in. They also need fresh water and plenty of animals for food.

TIGERS OF THE WORLD

Subspecies name	Where found	Population
Chinese tiger *Panthera tigris amoyensis*	China	about 40
Siberian tiger *Panthera tigris altaica*	China, Korea, USSR	200-300
Bali tiger *Panthera tigris balica*	Bali	extinct since 1950
Indo–chinese tiger *Panthera tigris corbetti*	Burma, Laos, Cambodia, Thailand, Vietnam, Malaysia	about 1500
Javan tiger *Panthera tigris sondaica*	Java	extinct since 1979
Sumatran tiger *Panthera tigris sumatrae*	Sumatra	about 650
Indian or Bengal tiger *Panthera tigris tigris*	India, Burma Nepal, China, Bangladesh	about 5500
Caspian tiger *Panthera tigris virgata*	Afghanistan, Iran, Turkey, USSR	extinct since 1965
		total 7500-8000

Based on estimates in *Tigers of the World* eds
R.L. Tilson & U.S. Seal (Noyes, 1987).

TIGERS IN THE WILD

Tigers are predators. That means they hunt other animals for food. They usually hunt deer and wild pigs, but they will also eat monkeys, birds and even insects or crabs. Tigers are so strong that they often kill Indian bison. These wild cattle may weigh up to seven times as much as a tiger.

This tigress has just killed a chital, or spotted deer.

Tigers hunt mostly at night. They catch their **prey** by stalking them, which means that a tiger creeps up slowly and silently, using dense bushes as cover. When it is close enough, a tiger charges and knocks the surprised animal to the ground. Then it kills the animal quickly, using its sharp **canine teeth** to bite the animal's neck or throat.

You can clearly see the long, sharp canine teeth of this yawning tiger.

In the wild, adult (fully-grown) tigers spend much of their time alone. Sometimes people see a **tigress** with her cubs, or a male and female tiger together during their courtship. Each tiger spends most of its time in a certain area of land called a **territory**. It stays in its territory to catch prey, to drink and to rest during the day.

Unlike most other species of cats, tigers love water. Sometimes they spend hours in a pool in their territory.

A male tiger has a very large territory. A female's territory covers about 8 square miles (20 sq km), while a male's covers up to 40 square miles (100 sq km).

A tigress needs an area with enough prey to feed herself and her family of cubs. The male tiger does not usually help to bring up his cubs. Instead, he **mates** with as many females as possible, so that many new cubs will be born. So his territory must be large enough to contain the territories of several females.

An Indian tigress patrols dry grassland in her territory.

Tigers scent-mark their territories by spraying **urine** onto trees or grass. They also leave their droppings in places where they can easily be seen. The urine marks smell very strong and may last for several weeks. Each tiger has a slightly different smell. When one tiger smells another tiger's scent marks, it knows that it is in another tiger's territory, so it does not stay very long.

Tigers make strange faces when they smell each other's scent.

HOW BIG IS A TIGER?

Subspecies name		Males	Females
Indian or Bengal tiger	length (head to tail)	9 – 10 ft (2.7 – 3.1 m)	8 – 9 ft (2.4 – 2.8 m)
	weight	400 – 573 lb (180 – 260 kg)	285 – 350 lb (130 – 160 kg)
	shoulder height	3 ft (0.9 m)	3 ft (0.9 m)
Siberian tiger	length (head to tail)	up to 13 ft (4 m)	
	weight	up to 838 lb (380 kg)	
	shoulder height	3 ft (0.9 m)	

TIGERS AND THEIR YOUNG

Tigers are ready to mate when they are three to four years old. A male tiger can tell whether a tigress is ready to mate from the scent she leaves. After mating, a tigress carries the young inside her body for about three months before they are born.

Right *People rarely see tigers mating in the wild.*

A male and female tiger may spend several days courting.

In the wild, a tigress usually gives birth to a **litter** of three or four cubs. They are tiny, blind and helpless, weighing about 4 pounds (2 kg) each. The tiger cubs spend their first four to eight weeks of life hidden away in a den, usually in a cave or a hollow tree, or among thick bushes. The cubs need to be well hidden because leopards, hyenas, jackals, and even other tigers, will eat young tigers.

At this time, a tigress has to work very hard. She must find enough food for herself without straying too far from the den, because she must return often to feed milk to her cubs. This is called suckling. The cubs will need her milk until they are about five months old.

Many tiger cubs die in their first few months of life, so this wild tigress has done well to raise a family of three.

Tiger cubs may start to eat meat when they are six weeks old. Soon after this they leave the den and follow their mother. They hide in dense bushes while their mother hunts. Then they join her to eat the dead animal.

When they are about six months old, the cubs begin to go hunting with their mother.

Right *If a tigress dies, her cubs are left helpless. This orphan cub was saved by people.*

All young tigers must learn how to hide in the long grass when they stalk their prey.

As the cubs grow older, their mother teaches them new things. These young tigers are finding out about water.

Over the next year or so, they will learn how to hunt for themselves. The tigress may help them by bringing down the prey animal for them. Then she stands back and lets the cubs learn how to kill the animal quickly.

When the cubs are about two years of age, they leave their mother for good. Now each young tiger must set up a territory and learn to survive on its own.

WHY ARE TIGERS RARE?

Thousands of years ago in Asia, humans and tigers hunted the same animals for food. People began to hunt tigers because of this. At first tigers were killed with spears or bows and arrows. The men hunting them either went on foot or rode elephants or horses. But the tigers knew their territories so well that they could escape easily.

When guns were invented, killing tigers became much easier. Tiger-hunting became a sport for rich people who liked to display the tigers' beautiful skins in their homes.

Sumatran tigers have become very rare because of hunting. Today only a few hundred survive in the wild.

These people are stuffing the skins of dead tigers and leopards. Today in most countries it is against the law to sell the skins of rare animals like tigers. However, some people still trap tigers to sell their skins.

Many people traveled from Europe to India to shoot tigers. At the start of a hunt, local people or servants rounded up all the tigers in an area. The tigers were then driven toward the place where the hunters waited with their guns. Up to a hundred tigers could be shot on one hunting trip. As more and more tigers were shot, they became rare.

Right *Often tigers appear on religious ornaments such as this Hindu sculpture.*

Also, tigers have become rare because their forest homes have been destroyed. Over the past hundred years or so, the number of people living in Asia has grown greatly. The forests where the tigers live have been cut down to make way for farms and villages. In Southeast Asia large areas of tropical forest have been felled because the wood from tropical trees is very valuable.

A tiger in the lush vegetation of an Asian forest.

As the forests disappeared, the tigers and other animals that lived in them had less room to live. Often they moved to small areas of untouched forest. But even there, the tigers were not safe. People still shot or poisoned tigers because they thought they were pests. This is because tigers living at the edges of natural forests will sometimes kill domestic animals such as cattle or donkeys. Also, some tigers that are too old or too ill to catch wild animals may learn to attack and eat people.

As hunting and forest destruction continued, tigers became rarer and rarer. For a while, it looked as though they would very soon become extinct.

These Indian forests are being cleared to make way for tea plantations. Tigers need forests like these.

SAVING TIGERS

By 1900, some people had realized that tigers were becoming rare in India. But before anything could be done to protect tigers, India became involved in World War II. During all the confusion caused by the war, people kept on hunting tigers and clearing forests.

It was not until 1969 that many tiger experts went to New Delhi in India to talk about tiger **conservation**.

In 1969 wild tigers were called an endangered species.

Every tiger has slightly different pugmarks (footprints). In India, people have used tiger pugmarks as a method for counting tigers.

These people belonged to two wildlife **charities**: the International Union for the Conservation of Nature (IUCN for short) and the World Wildlife Fund (WWF). At the meeting in India, the tiger experts declared the tiger an **endangered species** and decided it should be listed in the IUCN's Red Data Books. The Red Data Books contain lists of all the species of animals and plants in the world that are in danger of dying out.

After this meeting, many of the countries where tigers still lived passed laws to ban tiger-hunting.

Soon afterward, a population count of tigers was carried out in India. The results came as a shock: only 1,827 tigers were left in India! The total world population of tigers was thought to be as low as 5,000. In 1930, there were about 100,000 tigers in the world; tiger numbers had fallen to the danger point in just forty years.

If tigers were to be saved then something had to be done quickly. One man called Guy Mountfort worked very hard to save the tiger. He persuaded the IUCN and the WWF to raise money to protect tigers. In 1972 they launched a **campaign** called "Operation Tiger." Posters were made, to show people how rare tigers had become and to ask people to give money to save them. Operation Tiger was a great success – over a million dollars were raised worldwide to help save tigers.

In 1975 David Shepherd gave this beautiful painting to WWF, to be sold to raise money for Operation Tiger. The photograph shows the artist with Mrs. Gandhi, former Prime Minister of India.

This notice clearly tells people what they are not allowed to do in a tiger reserve.

Meanwhile, Guy Mountfort and other people who worked for the WWF visited the leaders of the countries where tigers still lived. First they visited India, Bangladesh and Nepal. They wanted these countries to set up some tiger reserves. These were to be areas of natural forest where tigers could be safe from shooting and from forest destruction.

The money from Operation Tiger would be used to provide equipment for these tiger reserves.

All three countries began to set up tiger reserves. India called its tiger-protection program "Project Tiger" and set up nine reserves immediately. These reserves were in areas that still had good numbers of tigers.

A tiger guards his territory in Ranthambhore Tiger Reserve, India.

Wildlife workers explored each new reserve, to find out how many tigers lived there and also what other animals and plants were in the reserve area. Local people were paid to guard the tigers and other wildlife from **poachers**. Even though tigers were now protected by law, some thoughtless people would still pay high prices for their skins.

Above *Gray langur monkeys are common in the Indian tiger reserves.*

Some of the money raised by Project Tiger was used to pay for wardens to guard the reserves. Some wardens drive WWF trucks around the tiger reserves.

Like many cats, tigers spend a good deal of the daytime resting. In the reserves they can relax in safety.

Today there are eighteen tiger reserves in India, and many other tiger reserves in almost all the countries where tigers still live. Within many of these reserves tigers have become much less shy because people no longer shoot them. People quite often see tigers lying out in the open, or even hunting, during daylight. Scientists have learned much more about tigers through watching them in the reserves.

The Indian tiger reserves have become a great tourist attraction. People from all over the world visit India to see the beautiful wild tigers.

THE FUTURE FOR TIGERS

So far, the campaign to save tigers from extinction has been a great success. Today scientists think that there are twice as many tigers living in the reserves as there were twenty years ago.

Does this mean that tigers are no longer in danger? Unfortunately not. More and more people are living in the countries where tigers are found. All these extra people

Tigers need plenty of space to enjoy their active life.

need space to live and grow food. So the natural forests are still being cleared and this is bad news for tigers. Soon the only areas left for them may be the reserves.

Tigers need plenty of space. Many of the reserves are too small for a large number of tigers. Where there is only a small tiger population, the animals are in danger of becoming inbred. This happens when animals mate with a close relative, and they have weak babies.

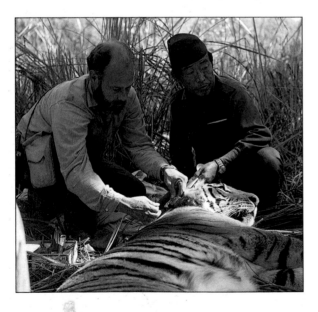

This wild tigress has been captured and fitted with a radio collar. The collar gives out radio signals, so that scientists can keep track of the tiger's movements.

If there are too few tigers in a reserve, other tigers could be brought in from elsewhere. Wildlife workers may do this in future.

There are also problems if the tiger population of a reserve grows too much. Then the reserve becomes overcrowded and tigers may spill out onto nearby farmland. Here they will eat the farmers' cattle. Tigers also sometimes attack people. So any tigers that make a nuisance of themselves must be moved elsewhere.

These Siberian tiger cubs were born in a zoo in Israel. In the future, tigers bred in zoos may be brought into areas where wild tigers have died out.

Tigers will only be really safe if the people who live near them help to save them. A poor Asian farmer will not want to save tigers if a tiger has just eaten his only cow. But sometimes tigers can help farmers. If tigers disappear, the animals they eat may grow in numbers. In some areas of India and Indonesia there are too many deer and wild boar. They like to eat the farmer's crops. This did not happen when there were tigers to keep their numbers down.

Operation Tiger has helped other animals, too. The tiger reserves protect large areas of tropical forest, where many rare plants and animals live.

*Some people think tigers are fierce killers (**left**). Others say they are beautiful majestic animals (**right**). What do you think of tigers?*

This ruined palace in a reserve once belonged to an Indian prince. A tigress has moved in for a while and looks as regal as a queen!

Every day, huge areas of unprotected tropical forest are being cleared for timber. So the tiger reserves are very important because they are protecting special plants that could help us in future – as crops, or as new medicines to cure disease.

Tigers are safer today now that many of them live in reserves. But many beautiful wild tigers are still killed by poachers. Fortunately, charities like IUCN and WWF are still working hard to protect tigers. They want to make sure that these beautiful striped cats will survive forever.

Glossary

Campaign   Organized action to get something done.

Canine teeth   The sharp, pointed teeth found at the front of the mouth of a meat-eating mammal like a tiger.

Cat family   The scientific name for this family is Felidae. There are thirty-five species of cat.

Charity   The giving of money for people or animals that need help.

Conservation   The protection by people of a species of animal or plant, or an entire habitat.

Courtship   The time when a male tries to attract a female to be his mate.

Endangered species   A species that is very rare and and is in danger of dying out completely.

Extinct   Not existing anymore. When the last animal or plant of a particular species has died out, it is said to be extinct.

Fossil   The remains of an animal or plant that lived on Earth millions of years ago. Usually the remains are found in rock.

Litter   A group of young born at one time to a female mammal.

Mate   To come together as male and female to produce babies.

Poachers   People who kill animals that are protected by law, usually to sell parts of the animal to make money.

Population   The total number of living animals of one species.

Prey   An animal that is hunted by another animal.

Species   A group of animals that is different from all other groups. Only members of the same species can produce young.

Subspecies   Different groups of animals that belong to the same species. One group looks slightly different from another group, but they can mate and produce young. For example, Siberian tigers can mate with Sumatran tigers, even though they look quite different.

Territory   An area of land in which an animal lives and breeds.

Tigress   A female tiger.

Urine   The pale yellow liquid emptied from an animal's body as waste.

Further reading

If you would like to find out more about tigers, you might like to read some of the following books.

Animal Ecology by Mark Lambert and John Williams (The Bookwright Press, 1987).
Endangered Animals by Dean Morris (Raintree Publishers, 1984).
The Future of the Environment by Mark Lambert (The Bookwright Press, 1986).

How Animals Live by Philip Steele (Franklin Watts, 1985).
Sharing the Kingdom: Animals and Their Rights by Karen O' Connor (Dodd, 1984).
Tiger (Project Wildlife) by Michael Bright (Watts, 1988).
Zoos and Game Reserves by Miles Barton (Watts, 1988).

Useful addresses

If you would like to get involved in the conservation of tigers and other rare animals throughout the world, you may like to join one of the organizations listed below.

Audubon Naturalist Society of the Central Atlantic States
8940 Jones Mill Road
Chevy Chase, Maryland 20815
301–652–9188

The Conservation Foundation
1717 Massachusetts Avenue, N.W.
Washington D.C. 20036
202–797–4300

Greenpeace USA
1611 Connecticut Avenue, N.W.
Washington D.C. 20009
202–462–1177

The Humane Society of the USA
2100 L Street, N.W.
Washington D.C. 20037
202–452–1100

The International Fund for Animal Welfare
P.O. Box 193
Yarmouth Port, Massachusetts 02675
617–363–4944

National Wildlife Federation
1412 16th Street, N.W.
Washington D.C. 20036
202–797–6800

Index

Picture acknowledgments

Bruce Coleman/M.P. Price 26 below; all remaining photographs from Oxford Scientific Films by the following photographers: R.A. Acharya 18; Jagdish Agarwal 11; Rafi Ben-Shahar 27; Stanley Breedon 17, 19, 22 below, 24; Michael Dick 6 below; Mickey Gibson/Animals Animals 16; Frank Schneidermeyer 4, 6 above; Belinda Wright *cover*, 8, 9, 10, 12, 13, 14, 15, 20, 21, 22 above, 23, 25, 26 above, 28, 29. The map on page 5 is by Marilyn Clay.